In Kingdom Gates: A Collection of Poetry and Prose
Copyright © 2025 by Janae Ballard

All rights reserved. No part of this book may be reproduced in any manner whatsoever without written permission except in the case of brief quotations embodied in critical articles and reviews.

Heart of Glory Publishing

www.ballardjanae.com

Paperback ISBN: 978-1-7350082-4-0
Ebook ISBN: 978-1-7350082-5-7

IN KINGDOM GATES

In Kingdom Gates

Janae Ballard

A Collection of Poetry and Prose

Table of Contents

TRUMPETS 1

Holy Transmit 2

Seek and Find 3

Witnesses 4

Firm Foundation 5

A Messenger Wanting Home 6

How Can Blind Eyes See? 8

What's Beautiful 9

Being Made As… 10

Day of Honor 12

March to Zion 13

God's Persistence 14

Musings 15

Holy Scripture 16

We Don't Deserve God, You Know? 17

Eternal Fulfillment 18

The Chorus Nature Knows 19

Stone Angels 22

Lift the Name of Yahweh 24

I Forgive You 25

UNITED GRACES 29

Residents of the Kingdom 30

United Graces 31

Edification 32

Today's Fill 33

A Body That Nurtures 34

Chastening 35

Of One Heart 36

Bride of Christ 37

Apple of God's Eye 38

Pure Dwellings 39

Best Bond 40

In The Cloudy Sky 41

"Triple Braided Cord" 42

This is Being Loved 44

Understanding 45

Resting Place: To My Brothers and Sisters 46

Faithful Family: A Remnant 47

What is Your Name? 48

Body Of Christ 50

a world for you and me 51

STORIES 52

Tell Me The Story 53

Sunlight's Love 54

Evergreen 55

The Kingdom Belongs to Children 56

Second Lives 57

God's Favorite 58

A Worthy Vessel 59

The Great Residents of Heaven 60

Sea Scrolls 62

Kingdom of Light and Darkness 63

Fire In The Field 65

Handiwork 66

I Will Show You Who You Are 67

An Immigrant's Blood 69

Blessed Are The Pure At Heart 71

Signs and Wonders 72

Birth of Bravery 74

Enduring Bonds 75

My Spiritual Fruit 77

I Am Seeking My Beloved 79

Mary's Baby, God's Ordained 82

Elders 83

Blood On Jewels 85

Entertaining Angels 86

How To Repent 87

Will We Build? 89

GATEWAY – THE DAY OF THE LORD 91

Seconds 92

Holy Refuge 94

Partakers of Every Glory 95

Ransomed 96

Reflections of Mercy 97

Full Surrender 98

My Friend—Holy Spirit 99

Enter By Faith 100

Ready or Not 102

Inscribed Letters 103

Formed To and From 104

Priceless People 105

Light-Shaped Key 106

Held Accountable 108

The Way 110

Who Is This? — YHWH SAVES 111

The Purest Fire 113

Snuffing Out 114

The Sinner's Grave 116

Land of Void 117

A Trumpeting Trod of Triumph 119

Purposed Good and Evil 121

Visions of Vanity 123

Blasphemy: Cake From the Mouth 124

Have you repented of your sins? 125

Final Rest 126

Splendor at the Gate 127

THROUGH PEARLY GATES ON GOLDEN STREETS 129

Gateway of Promise 130

Lion's Embrace 131

Eye Over The Horizon 132

At The Fountain 134

Loss—A Word of Mockery 135

Biblically Accurate Angel 136

Closure 137

No Worries 138

Marvels Again 140

Tickled Soul 141

Good Day 142

Village Victory 143

Fluffy 144

Toast of Wine 145

Golden Hour 146

The Children's Parade 147

Mother's Lying On The Wind 149

Do You Know What You've Inherited? 150

Endless Worship 152

Silent Night 153

XIII

XIV

1
TRUMPETS

Holy Transmit

You're good news approaching over the mountaintop—
a contagious smile.
I'd lay down my life for you, no hesitation;
I know full well.

Seek and Find

Go, turn over the terrain—
every pebble and grain,
seeking deep as you can!

Go, turn out the sky baskets,
clouds and rain driblets,
seeking high as you can!

Go, turn in the trees,
hollows, mountains, and caves,
seeking far as you can!

And you will not find it—
not under or over,
not even within.

Yet it was there all along,
having come and gone:
a Spirit, a Man—

holding the above and below,
the insides while out,
saying, "Here? No... I AM."

Witnesses

God chose a people,
set them apart as His.
But as all men,
they failed to keep the holy standard.

Many were cast away—many saved.
Now the chosen people
have extended throughout all humanity.

And all of it is mercy,
all of it is grace—
being called to witness
God's great love,
intimately.

Firm Foundation

Built on
mercy and grace,
Spirit and truth,
faith and promise;
On
power and hope,
love and holiness,
light and salvation—

Lord, Thy kingdom has come—
steady and firm, victory everlasting!

And we rejoice,
and rejoice,
and rejoice!

A Messenger Wanting Home

I am a messenger, far from my Father's house,
outside the place
my soul delights.
I long,
with strong appetite,
to dine by Heaven's throne.

I am sent
with invitation—
from my comfort, for your enchantment.
My Lord now
prepares a feast
and is committed to share the blessing.

I miss the simple joy of family,
who, faithful too,
carry these letters—
called to God's heart
of selflessness,
to take pride in the Commission.

And great *IT* is—
to come together,
away from hunger,
into engagement.

The wedding feast, in secret Kingdom,
brings eternal satisfaction.

How Can Blind Eyes See?

How can blind eyes perceive Your majesty?
How can blind minds utter to the heart,
"Send forth an utter from the lips to awe!"?

If the lake only squawks, and the mother is
not seen gliding with ducklings across the glistening mirror,
beak glistening wet with daybreak,
how can we reflect and not turn the nose
away—up from the noise and heat,
leaving the distant beauties passing by?

If the world only horns, and a mother tucking
her children in after bedtime stories
is missed by blind eyes, dreary from work,
how can we worship the Lord God's true image?

Who of us has thoughts filled with endless peace and praise,
if our pardoning Jesus is not seen?

What's Beautiful

The one who feels the wounds of another,
Rises at daybreak to serve a neighbor,
Sees a soul prior to stature,
Takes humility into conversation,
Listens for understanding, not counter statements—
For connection, not conquering;
Speaks of others with consideration,
Extends grace on their behalf,
Excitable, knowing how blessed it is to experience life's living wonders,
Moved to seek equality, eager to share favor,
Finds a balance in sorrowing, reasoning, and discipline—
Has a desire for redemption over perishing.
One who can build someone's potential while hating injustice.
Radiant wisdom, standing tall, confident and aware.
Knows the Lord with love, and cares for His creation.

Being Made As...

The God of Jacob is our Father,
The Lion of Judah,
Israel's protector.
We share His roaring Spirit— by it, we trample demons
   as we part and scale mountains.
We are being made as lions, and we will dine in the house
   of God.
We will break the bread of life, feasting and drinking wine
   with Christ.

The God of Isaac is our Father,
And the Holy Spirit has made us faithful—
Humble upon us like a dove, building boldness and fluent
   wisdom.
We are being made as serpents, but, through Christ, we put
   to rest the shifty nature.
On Mount Zion, we will walk among the creatures, in
   perfect peace,
With our Lord in great discussions.

The God of Abraham is our Father.
Visions of the Kingdom are bestowed to us.
With promise of righteousness,
We set our eyes toward Heaven and follow our given

Messiah.

We are being made as lambs, and, by God's grace, offer a living sacrifice in holy covenant.

And we will be rewarded with a crown in resurrection.

Day of Honor

Mine every drop of gold from our foundation and core.
My brothers and sisters are worth this—and far more.
Present them crowns and stages of honor,
for they shine with the splendor of my Lord!

Lord, the best shall worship and lift You high!
Humble-spirited servants to Your delight,
made kings and queens of every tongue and tribe!

Behold the days where we witness Your glory—
clear and magnified, under Your holy authority!
Your worthiness undeserved to know—
a call for celebration, feast, and confetti!

Lord, Your reign is descending grace.
Raise praises! Raise glasses!
Celebration!

March to Zion

Do you see the sound of color?
Can you hear its lovely people?
All the nations are returning to Zion—
in the splendor of New Jerusalem.
Marching in with tongues of color,
singing the language of their custom.
Robes of white rest over the city,
and it feels as northern lights,
and lays a quiet promise,
bustling out as clarity:
"The Lord, King, is faithful!"
This is what I hear them sing.
All the cymbals, all the trumpets,
all the parading tambourines
make for worship—make the music—
where God brings our voices to harmony.

God's Persistence

Where God
has set His heart,
He remains.
No minder of
persons. No
love refrained.

The one betraying,
the one straying,
the one resistant
cannot outrun
God's great
persistence.

What barriers,
what mountains,
what valleys
cannot be scaled
or overtaken,
should God desire to find someone?

Musings

Recite the psalms of David!
Pen new poems!
We will sing hymns together—
and lift our words of prayer!

Holy Scripture

Who should twist Perfection
and hide it beneath forbidden flesh?

Brilliance shines from Holy Tongue—
the permitted sentence is no addition.

Divinely written and manifest,
the reflection of God—Magnificent.

Christ's sinless heart inscribed
and given us.

We Don't Deserve God, You Know?

God created laughter, you know?
'Cause why are feet ticklish, and folks so funny?

God created taste, you know?
Royal fashion, lilies ate down. Yummy fruit.

God created ease, you know?
Did you forget—or think twice again?

God created love, joy, peace, patience,
Righteousness, faithfulness, kindness,

Temperance, generosity, gentleness—
And is everything that makes us happy.

We don't deserve God, you know?
But He's the Master who sent Himself to serve us.

Eternal Fulfillment

God knows
of the longing,
stretching over
the timeline
of existence—
the longing,
tracing over
every age.

He has come
to unite us—
our Soulman,
emptied of death,
and brought to completion
in Him who exists
long after old,
and able to enrich
for centuries onward.

The Chorus Nature Knows

The Lord has a heart that sings.
He laughs, weeps, rages.
The love of the Lord is deep,
flowing wide with inspiration.
His heart spreads across the shining, calm,
and brightly wild universe.

This is the reason nature calls:
it sings a song it's always known—
the clef, the bridge,
the whole.

A sound that fades, and knocks,
and replays unmeasured times
before we understand
we've crossed paths with God.

There's a beauty nature knows,
a great humming glory.

By the spring, consider—
and it will voice to you
that it was born to worship:
**"This is simply how I'm made,
and so it's what I do."**

If you are not ashamed,
tell how you learned the song.
You had to hear the Gospel spoken,
you had to read the lyrics.

Confess how you were out of touch,
until your new desires:
"All creation sings of glory.
Was your heart deaf to this Word before?
What had your eyes been fixed on,
and what are they fixed on now?"

I've since scaled cliffs and bridges
that I once had not taken.
This brought me through tragedies
and over slumps of sadness.

I knew I had lost myself
when I could not find happiness—
a chorus, long embedded,
a desire out of reach.

This led me to the edge
to pray for grander things.

Bridges burned, rebuilt.
Rhythms lost, revived for meditation.

I thought of God, and found
the meaningful joy of living—
a forgotten compilation.

Now I hear the subtle hymn of Him:
the hidden gold,
yet ever-present revelation.

Stone Angels

Stone angels do not draw their swords for war.
They are symbolic—meek women of the Church,
looked on, looked over.

Lady Wisdom speaks above the choir,
guards the room with gates of fire.

The disciples made, refined in God's shelter—
their heart a dove, their vessel armor.
A white flag of prayer for men to rest.

Their bodies: scarlet cords, bound with God on the cross—
but guilt on demons' hands,
whose thirst is their shame in second death.

True angels walk with men in visions:
God's male soldiers of surreal stature,
protecting the voices of the speechless—
a gentleman for the believing,
a blade to silence misogynists
who hate Mother Earth and her companion.

Robes of light reveal the wicked ambush,
the flaming arrow cast by Satan.
His weapons are divisive vices;

he seeks to conquer God's creation,
seeks to see His wife ablaze—
this plan disrupted during battle.

Hear the war cry once concealed:
the Holy Spirit—He is here.
Received by child and humble person.

The women born have been redeemed.
The sinful man is given second chance
by the same means.

Childbirth has brought Christ to dwell with us.
This statute moves the stony heart.
God-man unites for holy living—
the patient-kind, His welcome image.

Come and dwell inside the body,
unisex, unique in skill—God's handiwork.

Angelic songs of repentance—
the prophet and prophetess sentence.
Put off cold flesh.
Live in God's love.

Lift the Name of Yahweh

Lift the name of Yahweh
in every corner of the world.
Each measure of faith—
uplift His diverse appearance:
the range of spiritual gifts,
the paint of boundless glories.
Be clothed in the dance of victory:
flash the flying scarves!
With joy, praise, and worship,
form the rainbow arcs—
it is the smile of God.
The purity of Christ rescues
from the depths of Sheol.
Glide on revival songs,
float in hills and valleys,
on the merciful heights of Heaven.

I Forgive You

I forgive you.
Even when your tears were saltless, I forgave you.
I have always carried empathy,
as my own tear-filled well of hope.

I have sought mercy from God enough
to keep it dwelling at my core.

But we remained divided
because you lived divisive.
Shouldn't someone be angry at destruction?
There is no place for rage in love,
unless sinless and righteous.

I have not thought of you as irredeemable,
nor considered anyone's soul to be worthless.
But I am — and should be — suspicious
wherever virtue is returned with evil.

I set a boundary instead of seeking vengeance.
And upholding this standard is a holy, natural response,
and the lives this has and will save are testimonial.

I have been condemned by flesh to shame,
and guilted into confusion.

But the Spirit has gently sobered me —
that was not God,
but the devil's doing.

You, who — if allowed to reign —
lead to corruption and death.
Should anyone comply with you?

I won't.
But I will seek all our welfare.

Nothing is offensive in alliance.
But you hated me for preserving myself —
how I wished you would do the same for yourself.

I will never partner with double standards and
    misjudgment,
but with wisdom only.
Should we live a life of fury,
and embrace hell while there could be Heaven?

Maybe you have not reached its fulfillment,
but your experience is not my own.

I know the possibilities of God's ways,
and the hurt of sin.
And I prayed one day you would understand.

———

And now...
you seek me,
with your heartache quaking through your teeth,

apology breaking from your eyes —
now opened.

I also know sincerity.
This is humility —
unlike the falsehood you arrived in before.

This is the same humility I had to have,
to swallow the fact that
there is deep darkness in this life
that sometimes doesn't go away —
that people should fast to be free
and flee from.

Do you know how much that hurt me?
...
Do you know how much it heals to accept?

Reality is: we all wound.
What separates who we are now from corruption
is only painful admittance —
how cruel it is to disobey God's Word,
perfectly written —
and receiving forgiveness.

I forgive you, like Christ forgives me.
In my heart, you have every favor,
as if nothing wrong ever happened.

Because of your genuine change —
your redemption and repentance —

we have harmony
to reconcile with closure.

2
UNITED GRACES

Residents of the Kingdom

We have laid aside our idols and taken up God's service.
Feel free to remove the excess when you visit us—
the guards of silence or defense, the false image.
For in this residence, we are all known, all seen.
Again, you are free to show yourself.
If sin is confessed, you will receive prayer—
words of life. Therein, love renews desire.
We have access to God's grace
and so hone similar estate,
in reminder of His mercies, of the bleeding heart,
the wax seal stamped by the divine signet ring.
Come and dine in redemption.
Christ will be your first impression.
See it written: the angel's witness,
the Word poured out on our petitions.
The risen Jesus testifies in intercession
for our great existence
in the eternal, united Kingdom.

United Graces

Why does your being live for mine as if its own?

What tie of love was made before meeting?

Which friendships have welcomed a million gained and unsevered?

Who can showcase a more miraculous connection?

Where else do souls live in equal virtue, passion, and pursuit?

When now has unity exceeded death?

How can it be—

Unless they are wrapped in gracious glow and glory?

Edification

Edification pours like a fountain,
basked in and drank.
And I love you—inside and out,
through and through.
As the grace of Christ—washing over us—
is my Father's heart,
dispersing
His sincerest wonders.

Today's Fill

No more is needed than today
'cause happiness is full gauge.
'cause our cheeks are warm
and pearly whites are in full range.
'cause our bellies are full of laughter.
'cause sweet delights come in handfuls.
'cause we share secrets and keep pinky promises.
'cause we wear capes and rescue fallen friends.
'cause we keep playing after we fall.
'cause trouble has not made us wish for tomorrow.

A Body That Nurtures

I desire to be this for you:
A little guidance,
A little light,
A little rest.

Like a father's heart providing milk and honey;
A second mother's chest.

Carrying you as long as I can,
While encouraging you to walk and eat—
Following Christ and supping up substance,
To gain the riches of knowing our Brother,
The King, our Lord and Savior.

He is the Head, Wisdom, and Protector;
I am His body, proud to share my hand.

In His family, we're a bond forever,
Never having to let one another go.
We are spiritually tied together.

I will support you through falls and growth,
And watch you shine in the face of love.

Chastening

My heart is true for Christ,
but blind was I that night.
You sat as hope beside me,
'til I saw sight of light.

And the distressing hour of sin,
in which I was unrepentant,
was overcome again
by God's stern patience.

Of One Heart

My heart leans on your heart:
Their synchronization is as sound as rest,
And you speak from my thoughts,
For the same Spirit of Christ is in us.
And your tears are understood--
Both the hurt and bitter; The bittersweet.
Two souls and counting individually walk,
Two roads and counting in different ways,
But we return to the same mercy,
redemption, and aim.

Bride of Christ

Flower picked through thistles,
Do you remember the day?
You were delicately chosen,
Your flesh subdued by His name;
Your heart softened at His answer.
Do you remember the day
God gave you clarity that you were safe?
Do you remember,
Meeting His love—
In recognition that it would
Always hold you, has always held you,
And that you were always known?

Apple of God's Eye

Apple of God's eye,
do not cry.

From the day you fell before the cross,
you've been laid as a babe in the cradle of life,

where an entrusted heart circles
like a musical mobile,
in careful love watching over.

For on that day God heard tears of joy:
"Dear Father, Your sheep
which had been lost!"

Your Shepherd saw through a shared heart—
the God of lands sweet, of prosperous milk.

You're founded in the arms that carried you home,
and held as close as the blessed Firstborn.

Apple of God's eye,
do not cry.
Here Christ has wept enough for us.
But if you do, dear child,
God knows why.

Pure Dwellings

Purity of light
brightens the soul
and greatens the warmth
in dwelling together.

Best Bond

A friend who has the mind of Christ
won't neglect your needs,
for they won't forget to love you—
through war or liberty.

In The Cloudy Sky

> *TEEHEE, HAHA*
> LIGHT UNLIKE EGO

> *BAHA, HEEHAH*
> DELICIOUS LIKE BREAD

Airy, puffy, but weightless instead
The clouds
They laugh and laugh and laugh
They come in laughing
They fall out laughing
They go on laugh fading in the distance
That's what's got them all fluffed up
That's what's got them pretty

> *TAHA, HEEHEE*
> *BAHAH, HA*

That's what's got you smiling

"Triple-Braided Cord"

God's triune being
has been your favor,
your triple-braided cord.
But I come,
by the King's throne,
sent and sealed—
a soldier in iron,
made sharp
and proficient,
here to offer service.
Me, and my allies:
more eyes for protection,
glad to tend to your profession
and assure you take
no solitary falls,
whereby there are
fewer means to recover.
You
do not walk with fear,
knowing
you are not alone.
You trust God to intervene,
if He wills.
You—an advocate for faith.

We—could be that evidence
for those who don't yet see
how God surrounds you:
standing beside, over,
behind, and around,
to guard and defeat the lies
against your favor,
before they ever think
they have a chance to reach.

This is Being Loved

Thinking with closed eyes,
swaying by open blinds—

Light: this is being loved.

Dancing through darkness,
untouched by horror.

Understanding

A listening ear.
Patient to hear.

The shape of love
And understanding

A gentle lip.
An honest word.
Flowing elevation.

Receptive, construing
Equal conversation.

The tenderness of a heart
For intimate connection.

Resting Place: To My Brothers and Sisters

Your heart is a resting place next to my Father's house.
Your love, a fireside against cold terrors.
Your life, a light kept for company—to be known.
Your wisdom, familiar safety: a neighboring home.

Faithful Family: A Remnant

God said He had a remnant, but I didn't believe Him.
I was behind closed doors, seeing none like me.

He told me, "Go search,"
my whisper in the wind —
but I silently stayed near Him.

Two walking, until I could suddenly hear more voices shouting in the breeze.
Their every word, familiar, honey; I drank in disbelief.

The language from the heavens! I have,
and must,
find the scattered sheep.

I, one regained,
will share how I found a faithful family!

To those who feel left behind —
come out, and God will mend your doubtful eyes
and heart of agony.

What is Your Name?

What is your name?
We won't forget it.
It will be written down—
permanent.

"What of a name?"
Oh, everything!
If you take our last, you'll see.
Names have power and privileges—
the Word of God has stated,
and makes it happen.

For whoever is in alignment
with the Most High's enemy,
there will be no recovery.

But here, in Him,
if you are affirmed,
you have a great inheritance.

The Book of Life
is orchestrated as a will
to His children—sworn,
and officiated by the name
which seals earth and heaven,

seals the souls of demons,
seals the spirit of the righteous.

Oh, sons of royalty
and daughters of the King,
please know who you are called.

Your Father's is the kingdom,
all dominion and glory,
and He names you *Beloved*.

You are now bestowed all it entails—
by a name you live,
apart from sin and death,
forever in honor and freedom.

Body Of Christ

> I lend a hand to my sister;
> she's a shoulder I can cry on.
> Our brother keeps us grounded
> whenever he takes a stand,
> foot down in truth — imploring,
> "Look at their legs;
> how they tread so strongly,
> inspiring our race."
> Maintain a head of humility.
> We all exemplify God's grace
> and are in need of the whole body —
> meaning you, in your place.
> For while one rests, another is
> a mighty work to be witnessed.

a world for you and me

Friend,
I know some troubles are too heavy to put down,
seeming as though
they could crush the ground you walk on.
But I am someone standing in a different light,
and I would like to cup your worries
in my palms,
cast them up and off your shoulders,
release a prayer—send it off to God—
and make sure you don't bear a world meant to be shared.

3

STORIES

Tell Me The Story

Tell me the story
Of the first man, rising from dust,
Of an entrusted rib expanding into woman.
You always place your hand upon your chest,
Thinking of the world's first marriage.

Tell me of the ark of salvation,
And of the storm that drowned every nation.
You always place your hand upon my head,
Assuring wrath follows only disobedience—
And much, much patience.

Tell me of armies and crowns,
Of the sacrifices and falls of Hell's best,
Beating your breast,
And flailing your arms
The way that you do.

I love hearing stories of the Lord!

You speak them with much conviction,
And say, rightly so.
Tell me—
Mostly again—how it is all
Shown to be true.

Sunlight's Love

Sunlight's love
leads me forward,
coursing through me—
Sunlight's blood.

Garnet drops,
amber, topaz,
lit in the night:
a gemstone pathway.

Jasper rain
startles shadows.
Meteorite gravel sets—
Sunlight's torch.

Sun rays stream,
Dripping around my shoulders—
sun-kissed warmth—
Sunlight's love.

Evergreen

Mighty limbs and branches—
My son's an evergreen,
Planted stern and strong,
As solid as the Word.

My sure and steady fighter—
Who can knock you over?
Dare try, the beastly do,
But coldest winters leave no mark.

Your enemies fall to graves,
The mind's abyss of torture.
But you keep growing tall,
Trumping death and horror.

Rooted deep and firm,
Made to brace the wind—
The breeze blows in favor
Of God's land of evergreens.

The Kingdom Belongs to Children

Heaven belongs to the children.
It is full of wonder, but never of any danger.

Instead behold the glowing face
That has captured all throughout time.

None in doubt,
No moments uncertain.

God has a stronghold on taunting spirits—
A strong hold to protect the childlike spirit.

These young continue on in an unearthly state of being,
The common perfection of the new Kingdom.

They are bold and bliss, and simple brilliance
In God's fullness, immortal embrace.

Second Lives

    A lady encounters the supernatural,
then knows life is more than seen.
She prays for eyes of faith—
God grants her the Holy Spirit.
Joined to an eternal body,
now a new creation,
she testifies of a second life.

    A man resounds the same.
Once baptized by a flame,
on his deathbed he lies, born again,
with confidence and remembrance
of the other side—
the place of slumber and reward.
He testifies of a second life.

God's Favorite

You are God's favorite.
Your Spirit stirs incense;
Your heart fires fragrant oils.
Your prayers lift the aroma He adores.
You are the scent of love.

A Worthy Vessel

I don't have to worry much about you,
A drink inside your company, and I know.
I am quenched by your kind speech—
You are God's vessel, full of integrity.
Your cup—it overflows to me.
One sip is satisfaction.
One sip, and peace is known.
One sip, and my love deepens in gratitude.

The Great Residents of Heaven

Now is the moment for baptism!
And God has called many
to wash away their sins,
and to make room for the Holy Spirit!

I watch them purify themselves,
That they won't grieve His temple.
Heaven applauds their faithfulness.
How often are names vastly added to the Kingdom?

.

I am eight, and I believe my family
will flood through divine gates
to God's delight.

I love my parents, and the love is mutual.
God loves us, and this includes my cousins—
a quarter more my age, but a third to most "the children."

I have a twin, and others say
we're the perfect height team
for them to sport with.

These, and more, will enter, play, and worship.

Now I am reminded of "the elders."
We've grown around plenty
considered extended family.

I will count them, because they have been so close—
to me and to Christ—
like spiritual guardians.

A double dozen, multiplied and carried,
kin through Yeshua, His blood our binding,
devoted in Him and the Father.

And wow—God has more nations, Olympians,
spreading like the stars throughout the heavens!
We will be a grand and great residence.

Sea Scrolls

Replace the sea

With a dream—

So many unseen wishes

    Roll out the scrolls,

        Roll along the eternal fountain.

Fish the deep skies of Heaven;

    Roll along the breeze,

        Roll along the blessing.

Your heart's retreat is not the sea.

Inhale the summit of kisses.

Kingdom of Light and Darkness

I will tell you about two things:
Hell and Paradise.
Secret matters—not to be afraid of,
But to navigate wisely.

There are two kingdoms:
Light and Darkness.
Come, let's unravel the ways of life.
You are on either one's side.

> How do I describe the **kingdom of Darkness**?

>> It is the crimes that lurk in the belly of a shadow—
>> A murdered truth in plain sight,
>> Evils done and hoped hidden by the night,
>> And lies covered by the twisted *love* of morning.
>> The dirtied seeds that reap a chip on the shoulder.

> How do I explain the **kingdom of Light**?

>> Most hopeful—and horrifying.
>> A bloody hand, uprooting.

An exposition of fruit
And figs, blossoming.
The evidence of love—and its enemies.
A troubling witness's safe place.

Fire In The Field

You should meet my brothers and sisters.
They're most beautiful, in and out—
vigorous and of great stature,
and to them I entrust my heart.

I admire and love them for all that they are,
but I sense I will meet another—
for me to wed, set apart.

How will I recognize them, if not by the common appeal?
If not by their appearance or their kind will,
what separates them from friends?

But come—an interruptive passion to fight on my battle-
fields!
Once our rank and mission go hand in hand,
and we stand eye to eye,
I'll know.

Handiwork

Hands
The stunning task of bone and vein.
Watch their hands—
beautiful in strength and life.
Calluses would fist a rough rebel,
but the creases of their palms are etched in softness,
and their labor reveals love.

I Will Show You Who You Are

I left you over a thousand letters, over fifty books of love.
I laid out who I was before you, and how I've longed for your salvation.
The mansion awaits you—do not doubt My heart, beloved.
My rest could restore you.
The tables will turn for you.
You are granted eternal hope; to you this crown is bestowed.

Are you at the vanity table?
I will show you who you are.
Your troubles I have hated. Your tears—they are My blood.
What this world has brought to ruin, I will beautify in time.

Will you accept the King's honor? It is your choice to wear.
You are chosen for a mantle; I have dressed you in favor.
And what are your favorites, except that of truth and justice?

Have the jewels upon the marble taken your eye?
Or are you that diamond, refined through fire?
Hasn't your mouth been filled with pearls?
Ponder the wisdom, remember what you know.

Relax beside the Prince, your brother.
Draw your sword to lay it beside the river.

Enjoy the voice of a thousand waters,
let Him build you fountains.

Enter the countenance who knows you.
Abide beneath My wing; ride upon My shoulder.
When your gaze is set in heaven,
ask the Father what you desire.

In the golden mirror on the wall,
through the golden mirror of your heart,
see Me there, imparting mercies and life—
an heir of eternal royalty.

My words lead you close—
but faith is the wedding ring that lifts the veil.
Believe My message, and allow Me to transform how you view yourself.

An Immigrant's Blood

Have you been displaced,
Torn from your faith,
And the time you have is worn?

Get some rest
To restore yourself
And I will cover you,

Until you're on
Your feet enough
To lead and carry on.

If your thoughts are without a pillow,
And your head without a home,
Sleep in my oasis. It is ours.

God has given me a place,
So please come and unwind,
For where I dwell is love.

But you must leave as family,
Stay
As my brother or sister.

It is my heart
That welcomes you,
And how it will always hold you.

Blessed Are The Pure At Heart

A young boy stood on a tabletop,
holding a glass out to men.
He began a sweet chorus,
lifting his right hand high in worship:

   "Who has known one more holy?
Has there been one more pure?
All praise belongs to the Father—
all praise and glory.

   Who has known a greater mercy?
Has there been one more sure?
All praise belongs to our Savior—
all glory and praise.

   Who has known a superior love?
Has there been one more alluring?
All praise belongs to the Creator—
all praise and glory."

And the men sang along from their innocent souls,
as the Lord restored their youth.

Signs and Wonders

The layers of your eye
Hold mysteries untethered.
The half-truth of the sky
Reaches for fascination.
The Triune heart eclipses
A guardian's love.
The astronomy of night,
Consecrated by the sun.
Spot the dancing diamond;
Decorate remembrance.
You are worthy and more
Than the earth and heavens,
A wandering star,
A sinister planet.
Quite sacred like the angels,
Forgiven unlike Satan.
Blood moon, sacrifice —
Death to self and idols.
A puppeteered promise,
A shooting star.
The ruby necklace cost,
Seen prophetically:
Humanity under pressure,
Buried in the dark,

Sanctification—inscribed art—
Hidden pearls.
Signs and wonders,
More terrible and special.
The infinite hand of God,
The phenomenon of Him,
The fulfillment of our efforts.
His cosmic veil admired:
A gifted jewel, like flowers—
A gratis, rich encounter.

Birth of Bravery

Countless battles faced
began upon the knee.
Swords and strength fight nicely,
but the most vigorous Spirit
shall achieve.

Who taught you shame instead of honor?
Are they alive, or will they be much longer?
We have victory on the hilltop
by the prayer from the valley.

Now, give your hand to me,
and I, myself, to you.
Bravery comes after love,
and I can follow through
in a heart surrendered for you.

Enduring Bonds

Enduring Stance.
Cruel commands.
Corrupt rulers here.
There is blood on gold,
sweat in frankincense,
bitter smells of myrrh,
pain for profit,
prideful masters,
humble deaths—
the kind you wait for,
liberation from labor.

Lord, open doors for us,
refresh the heart.
Someone should weep for us,
but let tears be for joy.
Rejoice in promised lands.
The scorching sun wipes the face and hardens men.
The wrath of God has heard the heart.
The pride left to die has resurrected.
He trades the place of strength and weakness,
vulnerabilities exposed to the surface.

Light and darkness swap positions
on the earth of Hell and Heaven.
Where have you planted your faith?
On Judgment Day, the land will perish;
works shall reap.

Hand in hand, the black sheep—
bone of bone, flesh of flesh.
Nakedness, golden brown.
Marriage at the kitchen table
is a decision of love and laughter.
Who can be trusted wholeheartedly?
To thee can I give my entirety?
Wedding day repeats like treasure on the field of slavery:
a flash of Heaven beaming among mortals.
Enchanted by the breath of the one who says, "my lord."
Honor to the body and spirit that carry crowns,
held like roots centuries deep,
walking in favor, mixed like sunlight below the moon.
Victoriously free. Vows sacred and unbroken.

My Spiritual Fruit

Lord, would You like a fruit basket?
I know these are Your trees and vines,
but You don't have to pick them...
if I could gift You, please.

I will give my thanks to Love,
for His patience, for Your kindness.

How would You like Your apples?
I could bake them in a custard!
I could make You lemonade,
for all Your charity.

Turn the blueberries into biscuits...
Request a side of juice of any kind!

I could find You clementines.
Do You ever work up an appetite
in all the ways that You've been righteous,
and given me Your time?

I will peel and dice bananas,
make bread, so we could break it.

If I may humbly offer service...
though I know You're in need of nothing...
I want to give my thanks to Love.
It is a privilege to present You something

for all the ways I've been blessed,
by the fruits of Your Spirit.

I Am Seeking My Beloved

Have you seen my Beloved?
Have you seen where He has gone?
Could You be past the boundary,
In some new horizon?

How will I ever find You,
If You remain beyond reach?
My heart was not Your equal,
But You are not unfaithful.

I have taken You for granted…
I am lost,
And my pillows are saturated
By the rain of the night.

Your absence has become a darkness
I have slept to hide from—
Please, wake me.

I love You, but I do not understand love.

I should have never allowed Your departure.
I should have never treated You with contempt.
I have not responded to You fairly,
And now I am ashamed.

Oh, please return to me!
Has anyone found Him?
Things will never be the same!
My neighbor, share your insight!

And please,
spare me your porchlight
As a beacon—
my hope to know that all are looking.

He just might see that I am pursuing,
And that, like these, I continue burning
without true rest.
I ask again today:

Did anybody find Him?
His hair is the whitest wool,
His skin the darkest brass,
His eyes carry the flames of love

And the pain of a billion souls.
And He radiates
As if the sun were placed inside
A sepia water glass.

…

What brings the masses this evening?
These courts have been near empty.
Why so many people?

I came here only weeks ago.
I've wandered every city center,
And the streets' nooks and corners.

What is the reason for this push
And eager expectation?
What is this that I am hearing?

Who is this Name of honor?
I know only one miracle-led Doctor.
Do my eyes deceive me?

There is a peak of raylight
Gleaming past crowding arms.
I should not be found like this—

But You are Him—
My Beloved,
to whom I am bonded, and belong.

Mary's Baby, God's Ordained

Mary's baby, God's ordained
Fragile beauty, tucked in arms;
Ornate crown, spiritually embedded—
Holy ground: the manger's barn.
God spins thread around the cotton;
Mortal failure nips for blood.
God protects the history woven,
Entrusted blessing, Heaven's prize.
Trust God the Savior, through death and rise.

Elders

His ears are long, his mind is young.
Careful of his guidance—

a wrinkle of time has made one bitter
and another silent.

Choose not pride when you go,
but humility.

Respect men's age; seek wise counsel—
but trust only maturity.

Where is he who's walked with kings
without flattery?

Who gives to Caesar what is his,
faithful and hard-working—

it's the family man with
legacy in Heaven.

Read between each shaky voice:
is it guilt or bravery?

Listen. Learn. Don't rush along—
the broken clock sheds light twice a day!

If they don't chime with purity,
run the other way.

The hands' hidden hues are red
and do not point to Christ.

Does he stand on virtue—
or only with a cane?

An elder who is sanctified
is different from the dying man.

Blood On Jewels

You fought for the glistening crown,
To hold out your chest and boast—
Wanting prestige, superiority.
But once the public's need for honor
Climbed onto your shoulders,
You felt the weight of grave responsibility:
Blood diamonds.

How to lead, you did not know.
It wore and wore upon your head,
A madness piercing into woe.
You tried taking back your mind,
Taking a hold of yourself,
But staining residue
Was leaking on your kingdom…

A subtle revelation—
of what, or rather who, had true value—
Brought short-lived sanity.
The last jewel off your crown
Brought no time for recovery.
Your utter fall, before you knew:
Saving them could have saved you.

Entertaining Angels

Empathetic hearts
Can work many rooms
Can sow a seed of kindness
    Entertaining Strangers
Can reap crowns for homeless
Can speak medicine
Can smile like (and at) an Angel
Can be tested for moral weakness
And make the hosts of Heaven proud.

How To Repent

A window of ice separates a young man from a field of flowers.
He places his hands against the glass with indwelling sadness,
frightened by the cold touch,
because the day is bright and dancing.

He sinks in a blue-furnished room,
hearing the birds chirping,
seeing the paradise,
but feeling he cannot escape.

Ice spreads from the window frame each time he walks by.
He asks, "Why is this translucence torture a simile of me?"
The center remains a small clear appearance.

Somewhere within, he knows he should be transparent,
but fears the space would tighten and restrain him like the bedside.
Are not his feet and arms already shackled in a mental straitjacket?
Would not the walls grow padded near the exit?
He hyperventilates.

He cannot accept himself or his reality.
He will not leave the eye that says he is undeserving.

**If you find yourself visiting here mistakenly,
open up the drawer (as to say: seek out the Word of God).
The Holy Scripture says that you are not alone.

Remove the condemning "I."
Jesus is the answer.
Repent of the earthly master; focus on Heaven's way.
Take the one step that is clear — that is amazing grace.

The light that you have witnessed is yours through faith.
Be baptized by Holy Spirit fire.
To do this, wait and pray.

Do not dishonor Christ's sacrifice,
by which He names you worthy.

Choose whom you will serve.
Sanctification has begun, is done, is freedom.
The wealth you've seen is not to mock you,
but to show what awaits in His kingdom.

With love, God bless.

Will We Build?

Will new creation be like the perfection   in a chiseled marble woman,   a beauty that could never be sculpted by hands of greater precision?

Will we behold it, amazed—   struck by the craftsmanship?   Will our awe go on forever,   to find every facet and crevice of the mind   that gave us sight, and hearts to fall in love   with all delicacy born before us,   within us, and above us—   with *You*, Lord, who made us?

Or will creation be as perfect   as our flesh-and-blood Savior,   who first breathed   out the world,   and then breathed His last for its redemption—   the very life that goes on eternal?

Will it be as perfect   as the place He's gone to prepare for us,   as perfect   as the temple He's made in His beloved, who   holds the Holy Spirit?

When we bear Your image   in the new creation,   will we also build—   revealing the glories of Your heart and of Your hands?   Built in the midst of worship, fully built in Your rest and works.

God, when You say that new creation is perfection,   this
is accomplished in all of us.   And as You live—   creat-
ing more and more reasons   You are worthy—   won't
we build?

4

GATEWAY – THE DAY OF THE LORD

Seconds

**Here now, our royal family feasts
in peace, joy, and righteousness.**

Lord, You know some are found absent.
Who is deprived, and why is it?

Did they hear of the Second Coming?
Did they hear of the first?

Did they know You lived
and healed miraculously—

that You would return like the breath
You gave the lifeless?

Did they not receive Your message?
Did they not believe it?

Has not all creation
been Your witness?

Didn't we testify
to Your faithfulness?

Didn't all people
groan for justice?

Here's to
Your everlasting promise.

Holy Refuge

To marriage, wealth, and honor,
and all this world pursues—
your refuge is exhausted,
disappointing, too—
as you betrayed your promise
to keep me whole.

I am no longer fulfilled by you,
who left me empty and alone.
Yet in the darkest night, still wait
arms reaching out for me.

To every soul I tied myself,
only to break
at the sever of death,
or when your kiss of life
sealed its lips
and turned even the cheek away,

as you betrayed your promise
to be reliable. Yet breathing still
is a light, like gracious wind—
a kiss of grace.

God remains an everlasting Love and hiding place.

Partakers of Every Glory

God's masterpiece creation:
Christ—centerpiece perfection,
Mankind—carved in His image.
The veil, pierced by Holy Spirit.

This gift that we are given:

Strength of a ruling lion,
Heaven's water and fire—
We are fountains of the sun,
The Furnace's passion.

We mirror His reflection.

From helping hand and service,
To being set apart for justice—
We are, and will be,
Partakers of every glory.

Ransomed

For all our words misspoken,
for all our actions misguided,
whatever mishap or misconduct,
whenever we are mistaken—

God makes no mistakes.

I am loved,
and you are too.

He's sufficient for misfortune
and will chasten misdemeanor.
He clears misunderstandings,
and there won't be any more misfocus—

if you are ransomed,
and I am too.

Reflections of Mercy

Mercy is a phenomenon invoking temporal speculation.
In the end, grace is reminisced.
We take the concept made flesh with rejoicing.
His hand of friendship erases shame.
We lost the reflection of sin, gone far by a river of blood.
We have made memories with Him, and live for more.
Selfless, holy honor is the final response.
Ongoing worship is what remains.

Full Surrender

Jesus is our older Brother.
He can carry any burden.
One evening, I saw Him wipe your tears
and told my sister how
you resembled Him in strength.
For to lay open in the presence of God—
His will to pray,
painfully embraced and done—
is a full surrender
many cannot bear.

My Friend—Holy Spirit

I found my way into the Kingdom
By a very faithful Friend.
He came when I was lost;
He turned me from deceit.

His right and will picked me up;
He taught me might, and stayed.
He led me into fellowship,
A most amazing grace.

He has been steadfast and refining,
A love I had not known—
Alighting the value in my life,
Enriched by the treasuries of Christ.

Enter By Faith

Enter by faith.
Take it as the key—
The one and only way
To cross through the gate.

View it as the fire
Before a door of timber,
Knowing it can melt through
Steel and bolts of iron.

View it as the knock:
The beating blood of Christ
That melts the holy
Heart of God.

Knock in faith.
The metal ring and bob—
Hold it tightly;
Knock on the plated heart,

And you will be permitted.
Deny any other entrance,
No matter how wise it seems.
Keep this truth:

Faith is the way
To unlock the kingdom,
For this key is given
By God Himself to you.

Enter by grace.

Ready or Not

    A great fall of rulers happened
           A great fall of cities
    The mourning stages happened
           But we knew the hour was promised
    And we knew no righteous person
           would escape too late
    For it was the Lord God Almighty
           who called us to be ready

Inscribed Letters

I received a counterfeit letter, terrifying my heart,

an accusation of all I'd done to dethrone and blaspheme God.

All the accounts of how often my tongue ran astray, leading the life I ruled in vain—

even inviting God and all my good friends to party toward the depths of hell.

It read me bare, exposed it all, and by flesh I am condemned.

The prosecutor's seat is hot; I sweat and smell of treachery.

But the declaration of God brings forth a hidden page.

In the Book of Life is written, in ink, the memory of perfection—etched on God's hand.

My name and redemption verified, my Spirit foremost known,

my soul renewed and paid for.

I am no longer the former words; the devil's list is erased.

In God, through Christ, I am permanently claimed before the world of sin.

Formed To and From

When my life is folded over
And I go on to another form
And what I was is lost
I'll see you on the other side
Where life was hidden
And I am found different
From what was born
Changed for new experience
In what has become

Priceless People

Jesus knows—
and has shown—
how priceless we are,
by bleeding for us,
even if only
to redeem some.

So take this to heart,
regarding the blood
we've lost—
His sacrifice
is enough
to restore our families.

Light-Shaped Key

One light-shaped key of righteousness
Is Christ, divine to find.

The God who orchestrated time
Has joined His hand to ours.

Be known as His redeemed,

Be known in eternal joy.

Imperfect and forgiven,
A scandal brought to light—

Chosen through repentance,
Given faith to claim.

Given a Savior.

Given the God of love.

Given the Holy Spirit.
Given the eternal Kingdom.

Be known by the Father, Son, and Brother.
Rush into arms of love.

Be washed of your sins,
Be purged of blasphemies.

Take courage beneath the King.

Be risen with His glory.

Held Accountable

Who is responsible for the condition of my heart?
Do I instill the blood or the oil?

Both words stain the floor.
God wakes me.

**I rise,
or reset the alarm.**

Can you hear the wedding bells?
Are you the watchman on the tower?

**I fall into lies,
or pursue solid truth.**

The archer's arrows fly day and night;
there is no rest in relying on horses.

Can you sleep
during the angel's fight?

**I rebellious
or zealous?**

The declaration of war made moments sacred.
"Prepare for victory," the invitation.

Can you ready
the new wineskins?

**I faithful
or skeptic?**

**I divine,
and full of choices.**

The feast will hold men whose hearts burst,
yet assures their robes will be white.

Can you vessel the grace of a new day?
Will you be timely with the burning lantern?

The Way

Between crossing fields of straw,
sandy deserts,
or wooden bridges—
You are the cobblestone path,
the solid way.

In ways of deception,
confusion,
or having clarity—
You are truth
that cannot be shaken.

And in those ways of
death, birth,
and whispers of resurrection—
Jesus,
You are life.

Who Is This? — YHWH SAVES

Who is this
fallen angels and their minions
betrayed?
    King Yehoshua
    King Yehoshua

Who is this
seeing every intention
and contradicting motive?
    King Yehoshua
    King Yehoshua

Who is this
with ultimate dominion—in a category of His own—
by His own resolve, out of the void and darkness made light
and the universe?
    King Yehoshua
    King Yehoshua

Who is this
writing victory
and the definition of love?
    King Yehoshua
    King Yehoshua

Who is this
that could destroy
by a sighting of His true holiness?
   King Yehoshua
   King Yehoshua

Who is this
with heart to veil foolish eyes,
yet who shares His perfection with the open heart?
   King Yehoshua
   King Yehoshua

The Purest Fire

Before the gates shut,
there was a judgment,
and we were judges.
And I'd never known before
such holy hatred.

We each had rejected
death and sin's evils
in the old land.
But after we saw Him [Christ],
everything exceeded.

We knew love
in the most undefiled way,
and we poured out anger
as fire—
from the heart of His eyes' desire
for pure righteousness.

Snuffing Out

It took a while—
patience given for growth.
Fire had been given to refining,
sifting through counterfeits of gold—
the hardened hearts, rather than burning souls.

It took a while
to sow in tears, to examine fire doused.
The righteous are passionate fighters,
purposed for light—
an exposure for others to flee dark chambers,
to restoration from blindness,
how to avoid the devil's dance.

He needed more than charm to take them.
He wanted death.

But when evil does not blow out the candle,
lit again in Heaven,
the righteous live a long life.
(In grace, God may shorten a poor one of strife.)

It took a while
to witness God's image appear,
for men's hearts to pierce and glisten,

His Kingdom sought to come—
or be torch riots overthrown
by those who sold their souls.

It took a while for fire
to be discerned as help or harm,
the burn indistinguishable—

until the jewels were ready,
and thieves drew near again.

Suddenly, false fire was snuffed out,
and God's smoking flax—
inextinguishable.

The Sinner's Grave

God buried His wrath
beneath a lake,
and it boiled
and lit with flames.

It has been known
as the sinner's grave:

where the wicked
gnash their teeth,

full of hatred and grief;
and where deadly ways are cast away.

> What worry, then, survives in us?
>
> God beams the light of Christ!
>
> Appeased and pleased to set aside
> His persisting rage—
> to sanctify whom His Beloved
> justifies and calls His Bride.

Land of Void

a vision

Outside kingdom gates,
the air reeks of haunted men—
echoes of pain
from empty bones,
from empty holes and stares,
from empty apologies,
and grit to rage again,
to end the sorrow,
to revenge again.

Outside kingdom gates,
the air reeks of haunted women—
echoes in vain
from empty souls,
from empty holes and stares,
from horrified faces
with strained, bitter teeth;
a disgusting taste of sigh,
begrudging life and self.

a question

Why did our prayers fall through?
Why didn't You understand?
Why'd you place your worth in emptiness?
Why would you rid your chance?

a present exhortation

Avert your glare from death.
Flee the cage of scorching trees!
Break the burning lock—depart the maggots' graveyard.
Leave the land of void.

A Trumpeting Trod of Triumph

Blood rises from the ground,
lingering under eyes of fire.
Like early dew drops,
is a vapor of time.

Diamonds wet
in mourning,
refined for the moment
Christ arrives like sun—

> only moments before the chariot,
>> only moments after the archangel
>>> sounds   the trumpet.

The tares are torn through:
one by one,
two by two—

steeds blazing over
smoking skies,
raging hooves
kicking back ashes.

Tra-a-dumpt dump dump,

> **tra-a-dumpt dump dump,**
>
> > **tra-a-dumpt dump dump.**

The Lord's feet,
from the furnace:
on all He walks,
fiercely blackened.

He sifts for harvest,
burning all
but the holy remnant.

Sudden destruction
and patient redemption—
a millennium of judgment

> shared between God and His bride,
>
> > immortal,
> >
> > > triumphant.

Purposed Good and Evil

Angels are of light and darkness,
some with a thousand eyes on wheels.

We cannot see those who are higher.
Mankind is lesser than the angels.

God knows our every attribute;
He is higher than the angels.

Submit supplications to the Lord;
His obedient angels protect them.

People are of good and evil,
all fallen into sin.

We cannot see heaven,
while the guardians and the Son of Man are faultless.

But Christ has loved, and prayed first for us.
God ordains the final judgment.

People—repentant, marked, and saved by faith in Christ,
are risen from the lowly state.

The Lord sets the angels of light
to pour the bowls of vengeance.

Together, the godly display the design of worship—against and over a world of darkness.

Visions of Vanity

The snare is laid by Satan;
the test is set by God.
A lukewarm's temptation—
undone by holy love.
Lust, pride, and perversion,
idolatry and greed:
dangerous stumbling blocks
into strong delusion.
They masquerade as Christ,
but point to an unknown Savior,
enticing vain sacrifices.

Blasphemy: Cake From the Mouth

Give the liar the silver spoon,
The betrayer a golden room.
Crown man with the sun he made;

Let him have and eat his cake.

Let him lie on the bed he made—
Are the wicked not deserving?
Let the truth shake him from blasphemy.

Let the hearers find true rest and pray.
Let the devil find himself for prey;
Give him room to wake himself to hunt.

> **"All sins shall be forgiven except spoken offense against the Holy Spirit."**
>
> **"Out of the mouth the heart is proclaimed."**
>
> *Paraphrase of Mark 3:28–29 and Matthew 12:34.*

Have you repented of your sins?

You were taught about God's Spirit,
but are you familiar with love?

Is a heart too heavy to hold?
Can you take it up and mend its wounds?

Can you balm the weight of innocence?
Is hope the name you uplift?

Final Rest

One bright night,
Moonlight white—
A cradle crescent forms
For the second sleep.

One white night,
Christ-light bright,
A veil is lifted
For immortal youth.

Splendor at the Gate

Buttermilk diamonds gleaming from Heaven's gates,
Liberations hinging on the promise.
Prisoners of war, your bondage has ended—
Now, beyond, what inglorious shall enter?

Flowing as the clouds tumble forward,
Eternal joy and dawn surrounding.
The gates are stained with splendor;
Christ the Lord is here.

Marigold, the heart of Him—
The Lamb has bled a kingdom,
Shining Jerusalem.
Spirit's dream awaits.

The fruit of life like daylight beams;
Saints come clothed in light—
Beyond, it never sets.
The golden gates are open.

Radiant the path,
Entrance to paradise.
Zion's mountains high,
Anticipation near.

Heights of perfection,
Faithful honey glow.
Cities in the Kingdom are ringing;
Singing is the mirror crown of love.

Its royal shelter's sights to see—
Purity washes over new earth,
Like living water drips
From God's immeasurable, holy throne.

5

THROUGH PEARLY GATES ON GOLDEN STREETS

Gateway of Promise

Gates of promise open
to tangible good:
touch, taste, handle
the fruit unforbidden,
the bite after forgiveness,
the Tree of Life presented.

God's blessing is forever,
delicious to comprehend—
Earth's Eden in perfect Heaven.
Taste and see again.

Lion's Embrace

Pursued
by *golden* wings,

Gripped
by stardust's hands—

DIVINE
becomes your essence.

Licked
by *golden* mane,

Impressed
by sage's laugh—

LOVE
becomes transcendent.

Eye Over The Horizon

Lay here
on the shoreline of the ocean,
eye over the horizon.

This is yours—
every blade of grass beyond,
on land and in the breeze.

I hear you.
I made you.

Everyone will share equal rights.

Here
is an open door to creation.

Go,
by boat, on wings,
by trolley, on train—
however and whenever you please.

I know you.
I love you.

You rely on My guidance,
you visit My voice,
you have settled your house on Me.

Own all that I do.

My heart and desires
are with you.

Dear one, you are righteous,
trusted, and Mine.

Love liberates.

Here are the keys, silver and golden—
go with My love.

At The Fountain

> At the fountain,
> friends meet for refreshment—
>
> a space to shower each other with love,
>
> to soak in the healing waters,
> hoisting handfuls from their palms,
> splashing for laughter with every drop.
>
> At the fountain,
> they linger on,
>
> submerged in the overflow of their spiritual bond.

Loss—A Word of Mockery

Loss? Is this really a thing?
So—because of your foolish word,
our disbelief is ignorance?
What is *without*?
"Absence"! For sure.
Has this thought... *mm*... ever occurred?
Oh, you mean the opposite of gain?
Now I'm at a loss!
But interesting.
Truly, interesting.
Go on, elaborate on our so-called "yesterday."
I'll do the same for you, my new friend.
Christ's ordeal at the Cross
cast off His people's sin.
When death and vengeance met Him,
His sanctity devoured evil spirits.
Since we stepped through the Kingdom's gates,
what once felt like defeat
has turned to favor.
So, excuse me—
but loss is something known only
in the land of our enemies.

Biblically Accurate Angel

Life is breathed into mankind again.
Brick by brick, righteous—
the floor, cemented gold;
royal, flesh and bone.

And the nausea is swallowed.
The terrible framework of an angel,
declaring *"Fear not,"* remains spectacle—
becomes friend.

The kindness between the unseen,
the ghosts holy, the dark cloud dispersing—
it's a brave new world,
with the reputation of Christ upon my head.

Old earth vanishes with renewed mind.
The crown, beacon, the biblically accurate sight—
Love emboldens me to witness, to reverence
all the excellence of divine.

All the terror behind the veil, the confusion,
laid to rest.

Closure

My doubts have watched You be faithful,
and their gravity has broken loose.
Lord, You assured me—and it is so.

I enter the land of promises.

My spirit flies for You;
I gain wings through revelation,
now nearer to the heavens than ever before.

I am set free—and stronger—

because You've shown Your truth to me.

No Worries

Say, my mind is noting something I can't explain:
A vague taste, a most subtle reminder of forgotten things.

Should I want to recall it—no need, no worries.
God could write out the days.

So if He knows, and for me it has been erased,
That explains it is of no importance to me.

But say we take a peek at things tucked away:
The reproach of fallen angels, haughty demons,

And people reaping their given curses.
The hollow cries of vessels relentless,

Desperate not for mercy or justice,
But to be filled again in wealth and merriment,

With songs overflowing—
The cup and cry of innocent blood.

The drinkers are drunk,
And God's wrath, to the brim, is filled.

Tears unheard,
poured out in anger again.

Enough worry,
enough misery—

There were enough days.
Heaven

has washed away
The pain of former days.

Marvels Again

If sadness responds by weeping,
And laughter comes of delight,
Then worship shall never settle,
And praise shall be second nature.

How can our heart go uncaptured,
While inside God's holy hand?
What end of all wisdom
Does not find His marvels again?

Tickled Soul

Through the tickle, tickle grass of the field,
we sweep, sweep the soil with our feet,
and shuffle, shuffle the rocks with our toes,
then leap, leap the joy of our soles.

Good Day

Look up. Look around.
Has something so blue ever made you so happy?
Or is it the warm and gentle greeting of the sun and clouds
that makes you chirp, "Good day!"?

Has the green ever felt so neighborly—like a firm
handshake, welcoming?
Listen—and hear rejoicing.
The birds, soaring overhead in unison and patterns,
will engage you in their subconscious dance—
so clearly beautiful.

Radiant coordination and creations
abound in every direction.

Village Victory

Toss the daggers—have some fun! The battle has been won!
Trade your fear for ease—our marketplace is a thriving one.
We were exchanged water: a living hope, drunk for this revival.
Here, now, our sisters' spirits are high, and our brothers—keep them spurring!
Swords are sheathed in gold and swung for a hearty good fight.
The defeated fall with laughter; no enemy's stealing light.
Liberated on our feet—tall, up, chuckling peace.
Oh, the battle has been won!
Sadness, conquered in unity!

Fluffy

Fluffy—
the Father's charity, a chance to breathe and mend the Spirit.

Soft—
the atmosphere on Holy Ground cannot be comprehended.

Sweet—
the feeling of Love in a body that's transcendent.

Bliss—
the kiss of God, the innocence of agape presence.

Rich—
a heart laid gently on Heaven's eternal, granted wishes.

Retreat—
in a supple Hand swaying beloved jewels to peace for keepsake.

Toast of Wine

Today we drink the reddest wine,
the finest of its kind.
A hundred years this cork has held good,
but two thousand years (and counting)
seal the sweet savor of salvation!

Today we drink the richest wine,
affording all the earth's vineyards by its vine:
the blood that pays for our toast,
the crushed grape that purchased spans
of fields and bought away our weary labor—to Him.

Today we drink the ripest wine,
its quality worth more than galaxies of gold.
When a king's wineskin overflows,
and his glass never ceases being filled,
still, nothing dares to testify
a fool mockery's comparison
to what Christ pours out here.

Golden Hour

The sky glows warm at evening.
It is not gloom and full of ash.
It no longer bursts in anger,
Not filled with the breath of evil,
Not filled by tanks, lust, or greed.

The orchards will never be buried by the crying again,

Never singed by tears again.
We've reached the calm after the war—
A time of sunsets
Where apples glisten like the sun
Swimming in its reflection on the sea.

The Children's Parade

Marching with an Angel,
gathered for a game,
a little drummer boy and girl
lead with a skipping *rum-pa-pum*:
"The Children's Parade"!
On rainbow cobblestone, soft like foam,
all the saints encourage a frequent way of worship—
drummed up on thighs,
clapped to with hands.
A pitter-patter erupts
when the children spring to stance,
hearing,
"Stomp in place! We're about to begin!"
Whoever can whistle—whistle!
And you can sing and shout!
Birds and Bees loopdiloop a buzz or tweet!
Sunflowers wave and beam your beauty!
Bunnies and Turtles—keep the crawler scooting!
All the babies—christened.
All the toddlers whose families' faiths are different.
All the children—innocent!
For this is how God makes them—
a gift to Earth and Heaven.
Watchful and dependent,

curious, they mimic
the upbeat tune,
prancing on
and humbly praising high:
God is great, all the time!
See His face—it is the light!
Christ has put to death the dark!
No more fear, forevermore!
We can praise, forevermore!
Lion–Lamb TO-GETHER!
Father–Son TO-GETHER!
ROAR ON TOGETHER!
MARCH ON TOGETHER!
HOLY FOREVER!

Mother's Lying On The Wind

Mothers lying on the wind, adorned in flowing, cloud-canvas bliss, souls gently brushed and painted by sunrise love   Come—playmates galore, with kinship and friendship everlasting   The heavy heart is gone, restored through rising laughter   Under the theatre of Christ, toddlers spring forward, hand in hand, their lives glittering with glory   Nothing harms or breaks the flower   My nurturing friends, be carried on the timeless rhythm
These eyes, ever ongoing, now dance and rest with smiles

God is the hour's perfect home.

Do You Know What You've Inherited?

I dub you:
Mighty, unfailing, beauty.

I declare you:
Seen, protected, healing.

I denounce the:
Enemy, accuser, sinner.

I delight to:
Bestow, befriend, deliver.

You are My:
Son, daughter, beloved.

You are a:
Soul, vessel, human.

You are the:
Head, riches, blessing.

You are given:
Favor, name, inheritance.

Scope between My fingers;

Power inside your lungs.

Immortal fruit in the garden,

Held for the chosen children.

Do you know what is yours?

Endless Worship

For decades, worship has reverberated around this very room, where we come and go—back and forth—praising Holy's glories. A hundred years have passed, and the amusements of fulfillment have not ceased expounding from our ever-grateful souls. Centuries—thousands, even—have been sum and dedicated to devotion, to constancy in the foothold of the mountain of Him, where we kneel and inherit immense lovingkindness, inciting us to no end.

Silent Night

Hush and sleep.
Our silent night has passed.
All that would fade has.
The sun's day is done.
It burned through the earth.
While gold brazed with blues,
dawn went like a drifting field—
the last wind in humanity's lungs.
Earth sighed her release from vanity.
What remains now is eternity.
Below is a dark kingdom;
up now is light and sleep.
Hush and breathe deep.
Our salvation's come.

THANK YOU

With deep gratitude, I thank you for exploring the pages of In Kingdom Gates. It is my sincere hope that my spiritual insights, along with my passion for words and the Word of God, have led you to rejoice as you've read my poetic reflections on prophecy and scriptural visions. Piecing together glimpses of this beautiful hope we carry as God's children has been a blessing for me. May this collection do the same for you—encouraging your heart, inspiring your faith, and strengthening your walk in Christ as we anticipate the coming kingdom together.

God bless,

Janae

ABOUT THE AUTHOR

Janae Ballard is a Christian author and the owner of Heart of Glory Publishing, a business devoted to producing inspirational writing that glorifies God. Residing in the southern United States, Janae writes across several genres, including faith based poetry and fiction. In Kingdom Gates: A Collection of Poetry and Prose is one of her many works that reflects her visionary love of language and creative expression.

Readers can discover more of her books, ministry, and future endeavors at www.ballardjanae.com.

www.ingramcontent.com/pod-product-compliance
Lightning Source LLC
Chambersburg PA
CBHW030553080526
44585CB00012B/357